My Life In Black & White

Poems

by

Jaime A. Gonzalez

The contents of this book regarding the accuracy of events, people and places depicted; permissions to use all previously published materials, are the sole responsibility of the author, who assumes all liability for the contents of this book.

© 2018 Jaime A. Gonzalez

All rights reserved. Except for fair use educational purposes and short excerpts for editorial reviews in journals, magazines, or web sites, no part of this book shall be reproduced, stored in a retrieval system, or transmitted by any means without the written permission of the publisher.

International Standard Book Number 13: 978-1-60452-141-2
International Standard Book Number 10: 1-60452-141-4
Library of Congress Control Number: 2018938405

BluewaterPress LLC
52 Tuscan Way Ste 202-309
Saint Augustine FL 32092
www.bluewaterpress.com

This book may be purchased online at -
www.bluewaterpress.com

Dedication

To my mother the first woman I loved and to the other ones that followed on my journey through life.

Personal Quote

"He who races against himself
knows not the value of a challenge"
—Jaime A. Gonzalez

Contents

Farewell	1
Country Girl	2
Nihon'nobi	3
Loves Ecstasy	4
A Raging Battle	5
You're Leaving with Me	6
The Evil in Me	7
Day by Day	8
Woman to Woman	9
Remorse	10
Hurt	11
Feelings Unknown	12
Thoughts	13
A Letter to my Lover	14
No Cross-No Crown	15
Dancing with the Devil	16
Reality Revealed	18
Larisa	19
Letter of Recommendation	20
Lord of Heaven	22
Rear View Mirror	23
Being Alone	24
A Rebirth of Love	25
A Princess by the Sea	26
Getting to Know Each Other	27
You Are the Rose	28
The Mission's Trip	29
There's No One Like You	30
Nature Compares to you	32
Friends	33
Building Castles in the Sand	34
Lydia	35
The Master's Touch	36
The Princes in You	37
A Life Cut Too Short	38

Exotic Eyes Woman	40
Your Silent Smile	42
Cast No Doubts Upon Yourself	43
Daydreaming in Silence	44
An Impossible Love	45
Love in the Hour of Parting	46
Gazing at Your Photograph	47
Sparkling Exotic Eyes	48
The Red Lotus Flower	49
My Sweet and Gentle Angel	50
The Two of Us	52
Thoughts of You	53
And He Called Me Son	54
Death Cometh Again	56
Emotional Collage	58
Joaquin	59
A Brief Moment in Time	60
The Corner	61
Traces of You	62
The Fight	64
The Fifth of November	66
A Solitary Candle Sat	68
Mary Merlene	69
Second Guessing Life	70
Twenty-Six Letters	71
Unfinished Waltz	72
Lost Love	74
A Gleaming Star in the Fog	78
And the Enemy Moves In	80
Life O' Life	81
A Matter of Fate	82
This Old Soul	83
Thank You for Leaving Me	84
My Christmas Shirt	85
Going Off The Furrow	86
Jaime Gonzalez	89

My Life
In
Black & White

Farewell

I had a marvelous journey and God is my witness
I was looking for a rare gem and I found you
Yet today the cruel destiny dictates that I must leave
Because the traitor wants me to forget you

But I will never say goodbye I will say 'til later
For I will return and shower you with my love
It is very difficult to leave, and I can't bear it
Don't ever stop loving me my sweet ladylove

I will see you soon upon my return
Know you'll be living deep within my heart
I'll carry your image in my mind and in my soul
So that when we meet again we'll never part

Jaime A González

6-17-68

Country Girl

Of all the loves, I have encounter in my life
Yours my country girl was the purest of all
You became my friend right from the start
Till I looked upon you with the eyes of my heart

It was then that my heart was awaken
Giving life to something new within me
As a young man, I never felt that way before
I guess it was pure love, and nothing more

How my hand would sweat as I held yours
What was happening to me I didn't understand?
I was hearing my own heart beat
And immediately being filled with inner heat

Listening to the waves hitting the shore
Feeling the cool breeze rushing through my hair
Suddenly every sound was being magnified
As if the universe had suddenly come alive

Oh, my sweet country girl how I loved you
From that moment on life was never the same
For I believed that a true love had spawn
While no one has filled the void, my search carries on

Jaime A Gonzalez
12-15-68

Nihon'nobi

You confiscated my heart my little Nihon'nobi
With your long beautiful wavy hair at your control
You had imprisoned me and weakened my will
But with your exotic eyes you captured my lonely soul

With your childlike smile and your intoxicating laughter
You had me at your mercy at the very first try
We spent the whole night in each other's arm
Under a quilt beneath a moonless star lit sky

On the front lawn of your friend's house
We saw that dark night turn into day
I never thought someone as beautiful as you
Would ever give me the time of day

On many of the weekends I would hitchhike alone
On the Mojave heat thru dust winds and whirls
To see your face and kiss your tender lips again
I'd fallen in love, with the most beautiful girl in the world

Jaime A. Gonzalez
6-7-70

Loves Ecstasy

I stare into a reflecting bedroom mirror
Searching for signs to see or hear
There're a thousand voices whispering songs
As your enchanting melody draws me near
So, I imagined myself just loving you
You see what the imagination can do
It's not so hard to conceive
It's loves ecstasy, imagining you, imagining me

Many, many times our shadows passed
Seeing visions of new horizons
Setting the mornings light ablaze
And discovering that the light is you
So, I imagine myself just loving you
You see what the imagination can do
It's not so hard to conceive
It's loves ecstasy, imagining you, imagining me

It's a beautiful scene we both can see
You are the dream I've hoped for me
To alleviate this feverish fantasy
For day and night, you live inside of me
You are the living flame of love to me
It's not so hard to conceive
It's loves ecstasy, imagining you, imagining me

Jaime A Gonzalez
8-19-74

A Raging Battle

There is a raging battle between my mind and heart
My feeble heart cannot contain the immensity of that love
That has attached itself to it and has grown so strong
To the point that mind and heart find themselves at a stand off

It's a struggle, for my mind understands that your love is lost
But my heart cannot reason and it is only guided by its emotions
With my physical eyes, I can see that you have already gone
But my feelings controlled by my heart, still renders total devotion

An affection that must be dealt with before its total consumption
It's a conflict that will leave both heart and mind in utter desolation
So is it possible to make peace between these two dueling rivals
It is a bridge I'm trying to mend, before its devastating destruction

It's an undeniable fact that there's only one decision to be made
And as painful as it may be for me, this thing I truly know
Is not that I don't love you, the fact is that I care too much
And for my love and my sanity I'll sacrifice my heart and let go

Jaime A Gonzalez

7-14-74

You're Leaving with Me

Listen my love don't make me relive this dreaded pain
And don't put up a defense, there's nothing more to gain
Please don't cry, it will make the hurt too hard to contain
My farewell will be just a simple kiss and a gentle wave

Don't worry love, I know life may seem uncertain
It may leave you wounded, scarred, and beaten
But you'll be leaving with me, even if I left alone
I will carry your love, in my heart and in my soul

You'll be there with me no matter where I go
In every pretended kiss, I give, I would know
Don't you see that the tears I cannot contain?
In this bitter sweet mixture of blissfulness and pain

Don't say a single word love, for I lack the strength
To be able to say goodbye, when I reach the door
Just know you're leaving with me, even if I left alone
I'll be carrying your love, in my heart and in my soul

Jaime A Gonzalez
5 -7 -74

The Evil in Me

Being blinded by cruel resentments
I destroyed the love in front of my eyes
Because I treated you so unfairly my love
And it sickened me and I wanted to die

Those bad memories so often resurface
I can still see the hurt look in your eyes
How bad I had damage your beautiful spirit
And how hurtful were my despicable lies

The wonderful life we could have had together
By respecting the vows, I swore to uphold
I destroyed the sanctity of our marriage
And to a life of betrayal my love I sold

One abominable day I've always recalled
You were holding to the car as I tried to leave
I pulled away and in the mirror, I saw you fall
It is a disturbing memory I have always relived

You were carrying my child in your womb
What kind of sick man was I back then?
To treat you in such a vile and disgusting way
There is no human excuse for me to defend

So, did I hold a grudge for you leaving me?
No, not all, it just kind of took me by surprise
I didn't know just how much I would miss you
And being without your love was my demise

Jaime A Gonzalez
6-15-75

Day by Day

You probably never thought about me
However, I never stopped thinking of you
Never able to hear your sweet voice again
As day by day I died without the presence of you

Too many thoughts that raced through my mind
Like illusions of returning with you
To tell you that my feelings had never changed
As day by day I died without the presence of you

Knowing the physical distance that separated us
But in my heart, I felt the living essence of you
The way you'd brushed your hair every single night
As day by day I died without the presence of you

It is inconceivable that you can't remember?
All the wonderful memories I have of you
Playing board games on the living room floor
As day by day I died without the presence of you

How is it possible that you would imagined?
I would find the kind of love I had with you
You were my first bride, first woman I said I do
As day by day I died without the presence of you

With tears in my eyes I implored you to stay
But it was not what you had decided to do
While you returned to my culpable rival
I died as day by day my heart bled for you

Jaime A Gonzalez
11-15-75

Woman to Woman

I've often wonder what that first kiss would feel like and with who
Fantasizing about what it would feel like and making love too
There was something missing from my life and I didn't have a clue
Until the day this sensuous attractive woman came into view

I felt like there was something inside of me that wanted to burst
Seeing her walk slow in delicate motion, I was suddenly immersed
Her captivating looks and the way she smiled seemed to be a test
I soon realized I was attracted to this woman and she was the first

On our date, I felt I was in heaven for her lips looked so moist and tender
Her mouth was gentle and delicate that she made my entire body quiver
With one kiss, she calmed all those wanting desires that I had been after
I'd never imagined that another woman would get my feelings altered

I soon discovered that something had been missing from inside of me
It was not about the passion I was filling, now I felt as though I was free
Free to love a woman as I had desired, and the way I had believed
As for my first female encounter, it was even better that I had perceived

But the next morning I felt guilty and ashamed for being gay
My mind was driving me crazy, feeling my soul was being betrayed
But my heart will not be driven by what other people think or say
Only for what I feel is right in my heart, weather I am straight or gay

My mind and my heart came together that morning in one accord
I'm not interested in other people's definition of love to be scorned
It's my opinion and my decision on how my heart will be adored
Fulfilling the passions of two women in love cannot be ignored

Women are adorable on the inside, besides their sensuous attractions
They're tender, they're gentle and loving with no other distractions
A women's body is perfection to be loved and adored without hesitation
Being a woman I know, what a girl needs and wants without reservation

Jaime A Gonzalez
7-10-86

Remorse

Like a river flows through the misty woods
The memories of my blunders run through my mind
And the thoughts are like jagged thorns
That tears me inside as they pass by

Thou the past cannot be changed nor forgotten
No matter how hard we think we've tried
But the pain is raw and is very real
That it hurts and it makes me cry

So, in the loneliness of the morning hours
I relive the infernal life I gave my wife
I understand now what I put her through
Now I know why she hurt and why she cried

Deserving no forgiveness for my actions
Having no mercy to call my own
With this I will set my sentence
To live without her and cry alone

Jaime A Gonzalez
1-18-89

Hurt

The day for laughter has come to an end
As the gloomy morning began to grow
The clouds of heaven seemed to cry
As my heart became cold just like the snow

Cold and bitter like once before
My heart is turning like granite stone
Never to be broken by anyone else
This I promise to everyone I know

For the pain I feel now is very real
And yet it is my fault this I know
I gave my heart to someone new
But the hurt she caused she'll never know

So today I search the chambers of my heart
I asked God were you playing with my soul
But of course, He doesn't answer, He's not talking
What am I supposed to do? Dear God, I feel so cold

Jaime A Gonzalez
1-18-99

Feelings Unknown

Living with this emptiness inside of me in a crowded world

I long for something I cannot describe in words or vain emotions

Yet I know there is a vacuum deep within my inner soul

That is crying out for that which I cannot describe or even know

Jaime A Gonzalez

8-5-91

Thoughts

It is by far a greater gift

To live alone and in harmony

Than to live with someone

And be surrounded by sadness

It is by far a greater loss

To have loved and become bewildered

Than to never ever have loved

And not know the suffering

It is by far a greater pain

To be hollowed to self-destruction

Than to walk away ever so humble

And know in your heart, you really tried

Jaime A Gonzalez

9-17-91

A Letter to my Lover

I want to run my fingers through your shiny hair
Navigate the curves of your body with my lips
Caress the warmth of your skin with my hands
And feel the vibrations of ecstasy on my finger tips

I need to feel your warm and sensuous lips on mine
A sensation I surely miss and desperately long for
Admiring a perfect reflection of the person I adore
And seeing her face ignites my passion even more

It's really a way of having you close and yet not near
As I fix my gaze on the image of the one who's dear
Your hair your face your eyes your lips they torture me
Creating a deep yearning for the woman I truly need

So, admiring the precious photograph I have of thee
It alleviates that missing desire I still crave of ye
As I wait for that special day when you and me
Are united in a lover's embrace as it was meant to be

Jaime A Gonzalez
3 -7- 90

No Cross-No Crown

No cross, no crown
This is the way it should be
You can't bribe your way into heaven
You must walk the road to Calvary

No cross-no crown
Salvation is for those who seek
A man passed this way 2,000 years ago
When he walked the road to Calvary

No cross-no crown
He walked the walk for you and me
He carried His cross and scarred His knees
When He fell on the road to Calvary

No cross-no crown
It's the last time I'll tell you this
He gave His life and shed His blood
When He died for you at Calvary

Jaime A Gonzalez
2-7-92

Dancing with the Devil

So, I danced with the devil, in the spirits of things
Getting close to his mistress, for the pleasure of it
Seeking her company in the stillness of night
I traveled eagerly, towards her seductive bite

I was charmed by the taste, of her alluring poison
At the very instant, she sailed deep inside my heart
I felt her clutch my soul, with her insidious embrace
I became her captive, a puppet for her to disgrace

A strange weakness came and invaded my inner being
Like a parasite eating away, at my debilitating consciousness
She had me at her mercy, I became an anemic destitute
With no will to fight, I became a slave, for her to pollute

So desperately I resisted, while trying to break away
But her enticing magnetism, kept me coming back again
Hurting my loved ones, with vain promises and pain
Bewitched by the magic, my need for her drove me insane

She became everything, my wife, my lover, my friend
I thought about her constantly, and I needed her to mend
To be able to possess her, a feeling I could not resist
For I was not happily living, I was just being allowed to exist

Tempting and wicked desires, she fostered in my mind
Being intoxicated by her potions, I could not controlled
Weird and twisted thoughts, were racing through my head
I was between the border of the living, and the walking dead

My physical appearance, was changing month by month
For I couldn't see the effects, that she was inflicting on me
But as the years were passing, I thought I was in control
While in a sinister scheme, destroying me was her final goal

She gloated at the stage in life that she had driven me to
And her victory in taking me down, was not far from her reach
As I played her vicious games, traveling to the pits of hell
Getting close to death without dying, as far I could tell

Until that enlighten day came, for me to take a stand
Was it by divine appointment or just a random circumstance?
My dilapidated body began to cried out in a survivor's trance
As I stopped dancing with the devil, and granted God a chance

Jaime A Gonzalez
7-10-92

Reality Revealed

The love we shared has gone away

But in my solitude, I find an emptiness

Deep inside my heart which is tearing

My soul apart and it feels like life itself

Is escaping from deep within my inner being

But to think that another human being

Can have so much influence in the feelings of another

Is insane, and to realize once and for all

That the person who loved you with so much passion

Not so long ago, has suddenly walked out of your life,

Never to be part of it again, it's a reality very difficult

To digest

This is a reality, a very cold reality, but a reality never

the less.

Jaime A Gonzalez

4-11-94

Larisa

You were conceived by the act of reproduction

And from a tiny embryo limbs began to form

As if by magic you started to take shape

Then a heartbeat was heard inside the womb

A heart beat that echo in heaven's throne

For you were created by God and Him alone

For a purpose unknown to all mankind

And thru the miracle of life you were born

Now outside the womb your body shivered

Connected by the life-giving umbilical cord

Suddenly the cord was cut and you were shocked

Then two hearts, began beating in one accord

Jaime A. Gonzalez

10-15-94

Letter of Recommendation

In a very short time my heavenly Father
You will receive a sweet dear gentle soul
She has been a great and wonderful mother
But being honest and true is her goals

Her body is tired for her years are many
Inevitably is failing and slowing her down
And even though it may be old and fragile
With an angelic strength, she still moves around

And when the eternal sleep for her comes
I implore and beg of you my dear Father
To stop laboring for just a moment
And go to the gates of pearl to greet her

And if she convincingly was to tell you
Lord I am still able to walk on my own
Don't pay her no mind sweet Lord
Smile and take her to your throne

And help her travel the rest of the way
So, she can arrive in heaven without dismay
She would not admit as to being so tired
I know her and that's exactly what she'll say

She will sacrifice all for her children
Without a single care to her person
She would gladly share her last bit of food
With anyone without a thought or a burden

She is an overflowing fountain of pure love
That refills every lonely and empty jar
To know her is like traveling back in time
Just like admiring a far and distant star

For every wrinkle she owns, there is a story
Scars of battles passed that she has conquered
Of situations and acts which have occurred
And with the grace of God she will be covered

You are the perfect example we'll never forget
May God, bless you sweet and adorable woman
You have earned the love and respect of your children
And upon the arrival in heaven you will be summon

Jaime A Gonzalez
10-28-94

Lord of Heaven

Lord of heaven, Lord of heaven
Came to earth as mortal man
To redeem us and to save us
And through your blood, you made us one

Lord of heaven, Lord of heaven
Son of God, born to man
Draw us nearer, to the Father
And to the throne, of the Holy One

Lord of heaven, Lord of heaven
Prince of peace, O mighty One
You will reign, throughout eternity
And your kingdom shall forever stand

Lord of heaven, Lord of heaven
We will praise you and adore
For you are worthy, oh my Father
Hallelujah, evermore

Jaime A. Gonzalez
2-10-96

Rear View Mirror

I looked deep into her innocent dark eyes
Which reflected like fine cut diamonds
The light that exists in so many distant stars
And over the salted waters of crystalline seas

Her reflected glance was soft but very intense
That was being manifested over the rear-view mirror
Where I was trying to steal a glimpse of her eyes
As I became bewitched by her womanly attraction

Her appearance seemed young like that of a maiden
That radiated an aura of luminous life
I compare her to an angel descended from heaven
As the night was capture in the dark locks of her hair

I thought I was dreaming but I was totally awake
To imagine that image in front of my eyes
Perhaps it was a mirage in my sad and lonely desert
But I soon became enslaved by her reflected vision

Jaime A Gonzalez
2-5-96

Being Alone

Like the glimmering snows of a mountain top
In the coldness of a dark winter's night
My wounded heart does ache for someone to love
So painfully for her I search, but she's nowhere in sight

And so, in the coolness of my old empty bed
So blindly and desperately for her I seek
Knowing clearly that there is no one there
Deeply I sigh, and I cried myself to sleep

So, I pray to God for her swift return
To warm the coldness of my heart
But empty and cold, is still my bed
And sad and lonely, is still my heart

Jaime A Gonzalez

4-11-96

A Rebirth of Love

Out of solitude and loneliness
Was a love so strong reborn
In two people who ache with pain
To a love they had never known

It all started with a single song
A small gift of friendship I suppose
But there were strong lyrics in his voice
Words of love as beautiful as a new born rose

They shared a life of rejection and neglect
Unwanted and unloved by their counterparts
Until the day they gazed in each other's eyes
Unaware that at that moment true love would start

A love that would stand the test of time
Born from deep inside of wounded hearts
As you gave me happiness for a moment
Till the day that life tore us apart

Jaime A Gonzalez
3-22-96

A Princess by the Sea

The rays of the sun fell upon her body
As the sea breeze caressed her beautiful hair
Gently she walked on the warm sandy beach
Feeling free and without any cares

The gracefulness and beauty she possesses
Is unknown to her I believe
She is a rare vision to behold
And a precious gem to see

Her skin was tanned with a touch of bronze
A look that most women would desire
Yet she is humble in her own special way
It is one of the things about her I do admire

But beyond this writer's physical description
There is a glow that flows from deep inside
It is her love for God of that I am certain
And where the Spirit of the Lord in her resides

For her inner beauty is far more attractive
Than the accounts of her I have described
But you put all of them together
And she is a woman worthy of the prize

Jaime A. Gonzalez
7-18-96

Getting to Know Each Other

We must learn to be friends at the very beginning
In order to nourish a deep love in our hearts
We must learn to trust in God and each other
So, that no deceptions grow roots from the start

We must first seek friendship not sexual pleasures
In order to understand the needs of our hearts
We must learn to walk and hold hands together
So, that a true love would grow right from the start

We must learn to know each other inside and out
In order to lift the one when he falls down
We must learn to talk and be able to listen
So, that no quarrel can turn us around

We must learn to forgive if we hurt one another
In order to find real peace in our hearts
We must learn to seek to be friends not lovers
So, that in time we may call each other husband and wife

Jaime A Gonzalez
8-17-96

You Are the Rose

Please do not be insecure o' sweet little flower

For the Lord, has blessed you and filled you with beauty

And do not compete with the weeds of the garden

For you are a rose and the source of the story

You are a priceless rose, in the garden of life

Although some admire you with different intentions

Only a lover of nature will see your true beauty

And overlooking the thorns will love the creation

A rose is a flower which stands on its own

For it is God Himself who gives her its splendor

And you are the woman compare to this rose

So, lift your eyes and praise your creator

Jaime A Gonzalez

8-19-96

The Mission's Trip

The comforts of home we left far behind
Traveling west towards the setting sun
To a distance none of us had ever traveled
To a country and people, we've never known

The beautiful scenery of the rocky terrain
Was embraced by the sea as we drove by
In awe, we stared and could not comprehend
What the sixteen of us were going to find

Thru the winding roads we made our way down
Frightened at times at the precipice below
But we kept our focus on the Lord up above
And to the mission he placed in our hearts to sow

Down in the valley we saw the despair
Of the people who worked 'till their fingers were raw
No one even wondered or perhaps even care
But our Father in heaven saw the need to send us

Jaime A. Gonzalez
7-6-96

There's No One Like You

There is no one quite as lovely
Like this girl in the morning
As she dries her golden hair
With the gentle summer breeze

And as she looks towards the east
The sun it's slowly rising
Her golden hair starts to dry
As it begins to shine so bright

There is no one quite as humble
As this girl in the noon time
While she takes a quiet moment
As she sits alone and prays

And as she reaches towards heaven
With her gentle heart in tears
No one knows her prayers
Only the God who's there to hear

And there is no one quite as pretty
As this girl in the moonlight
While the stars of heaven come out
To see her beauty shine

And as the night moon is on high
Her aura slowly changes
Her eyes begin to sparkle
As they reflect the light

And there is no one quite as lonely
As this girl in the evening
When all her day is finished
And she feels she is all alone

As she sits there in her bedroom
In the solitude of her domain
For no one hears her cries
And no one understand her pain

And there is no one quite as peaceful
As this girl when she's sleeping
For the angels are watching over her
Until the morning comes again

And there is no one quite as lovely
As this girl in the morning…

Jaime A. Gonzalez
12-21-96

Nature Compares to You

The sparkle of the stars, are in your eyes
And the radiance of the sun is in your cheeks
The coolness of snowflakes is in your skin
And the tenderness of a child is in your lips

The enchantment of a mermaid is in your voice
And the silk of the gods is in your hair
The peacefulness of a dove is in your smile
And the serenity of the sea is in your stare

The aroma of a rose is in your being
And the sweetness of honeydews are in your breasts
The gentleness of a hummingbird is in your touch
And the gracefulness of a unicorn is in your walk

The warmth of the desert breeze is in your embrace
And the echoes of the night are in your sigh
The silence of the heavens is in your sleep
And the drizzle of the clouds is in your cry

The love of a Venus in your heart
And the desire of true love is in your mind
The hope of a better life is in your future
And the happiness of a bride is in your time

Jaime A. Gonzalez
8-25-96

Friends

A friend is a person who is very special
A person you trust and rely upon
Someone who is there with an open ear
To share all your burdens and dry all your tears

A friend is someone who is very honest
That no matter what, you would not be betrayed
Someone who is there to lend you a hand
To pray over mountains and turn them into sand

A friend is a person that you are very fond of
A person you've discussed about the problems of life
Someone whose tackle the worst life had to offer
And through victory in prayer they no longer suffer

A friend is a person whose first love is Jesus
Someone who feels God in their heart and their soul
A person so gentle and so full of love
Born of the Spirit and the God up above

Friends are people much like you and me
So, you see if we trust one another
There is no fear of being deceived
For we have met our Savior on a cross at Calvary

Jaime A Gonzalez
6-5-97

Building Castles in the Sand

The beach is now desolate and so deserted
And there is a slight taste of salt in the September air
While the sun appeared to be drowning in the distant horizon
I felt the coolness of the sand in a gentle despair

The sound of the waves echo in audible silence
As I tried to remember some years that had passed
To renew some feelings that were idle and dormant
So, recalling her beauty they slowly came back

Feelings from a time when the heart was young and innocent
The purest kind of love so undefiled and harmless
When moral values were far more important
Unlike the world today which is sick and shameless

A time when a women's honor was openly respected
And when friendship was the main foundation for all
When getting to know a woman was far more intriguing
Unlike the people today that confuses sex for love

Yet this is how I felt as I beheld her indescribable beauty
And how nervous I became as I held her trembling hand
How my heart raced when I touched her lips with my fingers
And how beautiful it was to caress her hair strand by strand

What a wonderful feeling to feel so young at heart
To feel the softness of her face with the palm of my hands
And seeing her eyes sparkle with the rays of the sunlight
Oh my, I felt like a child, building castles in the sand

Jaime A Gonzalez
4-22-97

Lydia

Her captivating smile
Held us prisoners for a short time
With her dark piercing eyes
She looked deep into the chambers of our hearts
Yet the essence of her spirit
Remains with us today
For we saw the love in her eyes
And felt the sadness of her heart

She wasn't dressed in fine silk
Nor her hair comb most of the time
Yet she was our very own Cinderella
Just a beautiful little princess in disguise
She may had been bare footed
And her body not perfumed at all
But beneath all that physical distractions
We saw a child created in the image of our Lord

I don't understand why she entered our lives
Or why would God put her in our paths
But I know she touched our spoiled hearts
And broke away the pride that set us apart
The vanity that we held within each of us
Was clear as a mirror for us to see
This was her gift to each one of us
So, embrace it, cherish it, and never let it leave

Jaime A. Gonzalez
7-12-96

The Master's Touch

A seed that was planted many years ago
In the womb of a woman by a man in love
And so, you became the woman you are
Slowly nurture by the work of the Master's hand

A delicate flower in the mud pits of life
Uncertain at times if you would survive
Through rainstorms and chaos, you lived on and on
For the Lord was the gardener and you were His own

Wounded and scarred by the enemy's hand
You withered at times but were always revived
Surrounded by a love you did not understand
The prayers of a mother and the work of the Master's hand

A sweet gentle flower with beauty so rare
Unseen by many for the blindfolds they wear
They look with their eyes and do not understand
That the beauty you own has a touch of the Master's hand

Jaime A. Gonzalez
6-9-98

The Princes in You

Once upon a lifetime there is a fair young maiden
Who becomes a princess in the eyes of a poet
Her beauty being accented by the gleam in her eyes
Which makes her radiance to really come alive

And as she moves through stale crowds
She becomes pure poetry in motion
For her golden hair appears to be dancing
To the mystic rhythm of her silent walking

Her eyes are brown as autumn leaves
Her skin is soft and delicate like fine velvet
Her lips are smooth and shiny like Persian satin
And her gentle smile is like water in the warm desert

Her voice is like music on a lonely night
And her laughter brings joy to a saddened heart
Her words bring hope for a new tomorrow
And an undefiled love that would never part

For the average man, cannot really see
For the princes in you is so well disguise
That they will have to overlook your physical attraction
And look into your heart without soiled distraction

Jaime A. Gonzalez
8-15-97

A Life Cut Too Short

The knock I did not hear on that gloomy dreadful day
As my elder son walked pensive thru my bedroom door
While pacing back and forth he did not utter a single word
Then the stilled silence broke he, while standing frozen on the floor

His voice seemed to cracked as he spoke these painful words
"Dad is about Jaime he is not alive with us anymore"
Questioning what was heard my feet immediately hit the floor
My heart was being shredded a million times thru to my inner core

My soul became frigidly numb as no emotions came forth
Uttering six simple words "What do you mean he's dead?"
My insensible brain could not process what my ears had heard
As I struggled to make sense while my wounded soul quietly bled

While we traveled to the location where his body was found
Quietly grieving and drying my tears as my eyes rapidly drowned
Tried shutting the world out to avoid the deafening city sounds
Searching for a viable reason why my son's life was suddenly cut down

Gazing at his cold body prostrated on an old canvas stretcher
Remembering all those wretched souls I had carried before
I saw a life that was taken to soon for his years were so few
As I knelt by my son laying still on that old filthy wagon floor

Staring at his lifeless body many feelings came rushing forth
I was overwhelmed by a multitude of saddened emotions
That were ripping and tearing my inner soul like never before
I screamed out an inaudible cry, seeing my son dead on the floor

The events of that day are engraved and seared in my soul
For no earthly father, should outlive the prime years of their son
Seeing my son, my child dressed, resting in an undesirable casket
Wishing there would be a way I could trade and change the outcome

Although some years have passed of that despicable day
The thoughts often resurface, of what could I've done differently
I blame myself for failure as a father, of not having compassion
But one thing I'm certain off, I did love my son unconditionally

Jaime A Gonzalez
12-13-98

Exotic Eyes Woman

Exotic eyes woman with your intoxicating smile
With your soft and fragile skin that intensifies your beauty
As your youthful serene voice adds to your humble spirit
Like no one I've ever seen in life or in any movie

Your sensual velvet lips cannot be ignored
As they are moisturized by a thin lite coat of gloss
Your face not requiring any type of artificial makeup
It is pure natural beauty, leaving every one at a loss

How is it that I am so fortunate to behold such a splendor?
That finds its way to the pupils in front of my aging eyes
Willingly without reservation and smiling without hesitation
Bringing happiness so long forgotten, and without any deceitful lies

Feeling the warmth of your hand being intertwined with mines
Holding hands together in those long and distant rides
My imagination running crazy as my thoughts drove me wild
Desiring something, I could never have no matter how hard I try

Respecting your sovereign honor that I swore to uphold

I live in emotional agony because I do know the outcome

The thought of never ever having you in my arms to hold

Knowing the specific day of your departure is leaving me numb

Exotic eyes woman you have awaken a dormant passion

That had been buried deep within the chambers of my soul

Feelings of wanting, feelings of caring, and feelings of love

You've given me the pleasures and you have made me whole

So, I will treasure the last few days we will have together

And I will try to make them last for the rest of my life

I will keep your image engraved deep within my heart

Where not even death can take it away in the afterlife

Jaime A Gonzalez

3-7-99

Your Silent Smile

Now the days are very long, not being able see you each day
As you were that ray of sunshine that seemed to warmed my heart
For I was greeted each morning with your soft and beautiful smile
A smile that silently transformed me and reenergized my heart

Now there exist a void, for there are no more smiles to be shared
I must now live with the remembrance of your sweet and tender lips
The lips that created an illuminating smile that I came enjoy every day
Which now must remain in memory for the sake of my hardships

With your silent smile, you had shared so many deep private feelings
That were hidden within the deepest regions of your immortal soul
And I was there as the recipient of your precious and tender affection
Which will now remain in my heart as the only means to be console

Where are you now, my sweet and tender smile which I came to behold
Forever lost I suppose in the physical distance of space and time
Never to enjoy again in the mornings of my awaking, or my arising
For your departure, has caused irredeemable loneliness for a lifetime

I will keep my sadness and my anguish in totality and anonymity
I will bear all the solitude and I will bear the constant suffering
I will keep your identity in my heart lock away guarded in secret
I swear your silent smile will remain with me even thou I am aching

Jaime A Gonzalez
7-10-99

Cast No Doubts Upon Yourself

Why must you doubt yourself about your exceptional beauty?
Because beholding such grace you may get easily overwhelm?
Through my eyes it is not so, for elegance comes from deep inside
And it transcends itself from the spiritual into the physical realm

Some women may view themselves as being very attractive
But their spirits may be rotten through to their inner core
That will nullify any physical charm they claim to possess
For beauty is not just on the skin but it filters out from every pore

It's why I can tell you with sincerity, just how glamorous you are
You wear no makeup, you wear no eye liner, and you wear no lipstick
But you have been blessed with a touch of remarkable elegance
That manifest itself from your inner being silencing all the skeptics

For you possess a face which resembles that of heavenly angel
So please, leave all those negative thoughts to themselves
You're a very attractive and graceful woman in your own rights
Remember who you are, and cast no doubts upon yourself

Jaime A Gonzalez
8-15-99

Daydreaming in Silence

If I whisper your name in silence, would you hear it in your mind?
If I say your name in thought, would you hear it in your soul?
If I kiss you in my mind, would you feel my presence on your lips?
If I think of caressing your hair, would you feel it in your dreams?

If I cry a lonely tear, would you feel the wetness on your cheek?
If my heart cries out in pain, would you feel the agony in yours?
If I lay awake at night, would you feel my eyes wanting to see you?
If in my soul I reach out for you, would you sense my tender touch?

If I imaging you in my arms, would you feel the warm embrace?
If I envision holding your hands, would you feel their warmth?
If I conceive looking into your eyes, would you be looking back at me?
If I perceive your radiant smile, would you be smiling back at me?

If I visualized this mental picture, would you say that I'm insane?
If I create this crazy illusion, would you believe I miss you?
If I had told you about all my feelings, would you still had gone?
If I could have that one day back, I would never let you go.

Jaime A Gonzalez
2-14-99

An Impossible Love

An adorable, impossible love has cleaved onto my heart
Slowly and silently inched its way to the chambers within
And there it lays causing no hurt and creating no pain
Mutely still, giving off a caring warmth, I can't explain

A love that can't be measure across the distance of time
Yet it stealthily exists in the vastness of our known universe
Unknown by the multitude of species who may live within it
The only exception is those two people who seem to share it

It is an invisible feeling which sadly cannot be express
For it may be looked upon as being slightly crazy, I guess
Never the less it lives on within our spirits and our minds
It's not a physical desire, but emotional one that us binds

Because it filled a void which was growing within my being
For sentimental weakness was steadily consuming my soul
Till the day she walked into my life, with a captivating smile
Igniting those decaying feelings, with her simple girly style

Yes, you are the one who instilled hope and gave me life
You restarted that flame that was steadily burning out
Because of you my spirit was reenergized, and awakened
You are an impossible love, for you are already taken

Jaime A Gonzalez
4-14-99

Love in the Hour of Parting

Parting has never been easy especially when emotions are involved
For it is in the leaving that we discover the real measure of that love
It clouds our minds with regrets of certain things we should have said
Now physically separated from that presence you're feeling almost dead

Dead in a sense that it hurts, with every breath you take, you're suffocated
By the inability to take control of your feelings, you become nauseated
Every place you go, only seems to cause more pain, and it's only a reminder
Of that presence, that has left a void in your soul and you look for an answer

To a question that was never asked, an answer that you will never receive
So why will you torture yourself, searching for answers that you can't conceive
That's the irony, for as long as you hold on to that pain that exist in your solitude
You get to keep that presence, and the feeling that love is being renewed

But it's all an emotional delusion, for in reality you know that person is gone
Will you be able to see them again, it's uncertain, but only if they return home?
Then will you open yourself for a chance of another heartbreaking departure?
Certainly, love is that strong, even though you know you will again be torture

Jaime A Gonzalez

4-5-99

Gazing at Your Photograph

What a relief to the spirit your smile does bring
Keeping the image fresh in the mind within
Allowing neither distance nor sadness to creep in
A glance at your photograph, my heart begins to sing

Like a summer breeze your smile brings warmth
To the visual appearance your lips transforms
Into a delicate picture of desire to absorb
An explicable vision too perfect to be the norm

Your hair so accentuates this living landscape
For every strand of hair flows evenly into shape
Those eyes so exotic from the Fareast states
That the beauty you possess will never dissipate

For your countenance is so well displayed
If I were an artist on canvas you would be portrayed
Forever capturing the heavenly elegance conveyed
Eternally etched in its new timeless form it stayed

Jaime A Gonzalez
5-21-99

Sparkling Exotic Eyes

Even though there are ten thousand miles between us
Nothing in this world can keep me from seeing your face
For there exist this instant video signal over the web
That brings your image directly into my private space

It is there that I am able to see your sparkling exotic eyes
Those bewitching eyes that have enslave my tender heart
And my only desire is to see your face every single day
Even if it is just for a single minute, before I start my day

For I have become addicted to the gleam in your eyes
It has become a need that I cannot seem to control
A need that only a glance is enough to keep me calm
If is just enough for that one day, until a new day is reborn

So, I have treasured the instant video time we have together
It is there that I found the solace and comfort I depend upon
Seeing your ever loving face, and those sparkling exotic eyes
That seemed to share your love and the peace to hold on

Jaime A. Gonzalez
6-3-99

The Red Lotus Flower

Sensual and mysterious woman from the east

How is it that you came to be so flawlessly beautiful?

Do I dare compare you to nature's own wild flower?

If I did, which one of the floral landscape will I choose?

I believe I have an insight into your spirit and your soul

I've discovered certain qualities that others have missed

I've looked deep into your mystic and enchanting eyes

They have revealed the passion that lives within you

I see the sensitivity and care that flows from your heart

For I feel its compassion and your willingness to serve others

Your emotions and your passion is a gift given to you at birth

In your heart, there is only love, you are a red lotus flower

Jaime A Gonzalez

3-20-99

My Sweet and Gentle Angel

My sweet and gentle angel how I've missed your stunning face
It has been a wondrous delight to look upon your radiant beauty
For you are like an angelic vision for my delicate eyes to see
Now that you're gone all that remains is a memory within me

A memory that will tug my heart looking for some image of you
Unaware that it will cause those feelings to rupture my heart in two
For you o' sweet little angel are buried so deep inside my inner being
That nothing in this life will be able to stop or heal that painful sting

This ache is raw and it shall remain in me for heaven knows how long
O' sweet and gentle angel tell me; how can I survive the agony I am in?
But don't be worry my sweet and gentle love, I can live with this pain
It's an honorable sacrifice I must endure but in the end, it will be my gain

So, I must live in pain while guarding your true name in total silence
The sweet and gentle angel who lavished me with such delicate passions
Teaching me that real love still does exist in plain every day expressions
Unseen by many people who couldn't understand those simple actions

You are now and forever shall be my one sweet and gentle angel
Who sneaked into my dormant heart and ignited it with a spark of love
A spark that had been deliberately extinguished a very long time ago
Warming the blood that runs through my veins into a radiating glow

No one in recent memory or even in times that have gone by
Had ever achieved what you have accomplish in a very short time
Awakening a spirit of love that had been sleeping since my prime
Sweet and gentle angel, who will be worthy of your love is this lifetime?

If I could, I would, but I know is impossible to even be considered as such
I was just someone who was able to sample a small portion of your love
A taste that will linger in my lips and my heart for all eternity and above
I'm so honored by you sharing a delicate part of you, my sweet ladylove

My hands will never again caress such elegance, radiance and beauty
Such an angelic face, that is so fair, so smooth, so delicate, and so fragile
For your appearance resembles that of a descending heavenly angel
Who came to my rescue in a time in my life when love was willing and able

So, my sweet and gentle angel, I will never forget your silent smile
Neither will I forget those sparkling and bewitching exotic eyes
And I shall always remember the taste of your sweet and tender lips
I'll never forget the experience we shared on the night we said good-bye

Jaime A Gonzalez
5-17-99

The Two of Us

Last evening when you were here laying peacefully next me
I felt so emotional seeing you, that my heart was filled with glee
It was fantastic to observe your joy and that wonderful smile
That I fully understood that the wait had been worthwhile

I study every inch of your face as if it had been for the first time
I couldn't believe you were here and that you were totally mines
Resting your head upon my pillow as I gazed into your eyes
I was so overwhelmed by emotions I couldn't keep my eyes dry

As tears of joy and happiness flowed freely onto my face
You exhibited a sexy mischievous smile as I was being embrace
I held you so close and so tight that I felt the rhythm of your heart
For I did not want to let you go, so that we could never be apart

I held you in my arms and sensing the warmth of your breath
You let out a deep sensual moan as I gently caressed your breasts
You pleaded, don't stop as your breathing became louder
Suddenly I woke up from my dream, got up and took a cold shower

Jaime A Gonzalez
8-7-99

Thoughts of You

The trips we took, the scenes we saw, the glances we shared

The hands we held, the words we said, cannot be compared

The clothes you wore, the scent you used, the way you dried your hair

The things I remember most about you, will always be there

The movies you watched, the songs you heard, and the books you read

The food we ate, the drinks we had, and the way you lay your head

The way you laughed, the way you smiled, and the way you got scared

The things I remember most about you, will always be there

For now, I think of all the things, that we ever did and said

They are in my soul and in my head

Thoughts that I can't control, will always be there

Feelings from deep inside my heart, because I always cared

Jaime A Gonzalez

4-16-99

And He Called Me Son

I have been called by my circumstances
Sometimes not by my real name
Some people have called me a weakling
Others have called me insane

And I've said some things that I shouldn't have said
I did some things that I shouldn't have done
Hurt some people that I shouldn't have hurt
But I called up on Jesus and He called me His son

And a wholesome God looked at this broken man
Not to remember the things I have done
And a healthy God looked at this wounded soul
And after all I've done He still called me His son

I held on to some things, that I should of have dropped
I dropped some things that I should of have held on
But because of His mercy and grace
He still called me His son

But you know why I love Him?
Because no matter what evil I'd done
He still forgave all my retched sins
And like a father would, He called me His son

He healed me from way deep inside
So, no one saw what He had done
Some people said, "Oh he isn't real"
But I knew! Because, He called me His son

He then said I'm going to heal you in the inside
Then I'm going to heal you as a man
I'm going to heal your reputation
And I'm going to bless you once again

I'm going to give you what I promised
A gift to cherish and to hold on
I have washed you in my blood
And I have called you my son

Jaime A. Gonzalez

2-3-00

Death Cometh Again

I've suffered many types of death within me
Perhaps you wonder how possible could this be
For I am writing about these very facts you see
For some deaths had cometh to set me free

Cutting the chains that I've carried within me
Forged by deeds that my mind had conceived
It was death that had cometh to visit with me
I've toyed and I've gamble and yet I still live

A death of a girl's heart when I was nineteen
I killed it with betrayal she knows that I did
So, death came by later and it laughed at me
While killing the love that my wife had for me

These deaths left sensitive scars you see
As I tried to heal them with new loves to be
Short lived lives and relationships indeed
Filled with broken promises I did not keep

So, death came by many times for me
Emotional and spiritual deaths I agree
Not to suffer that type of dying I decreed
And death show up again with a sinister glee

Killing all the loves I've desired for me
That sinister specter wouldn't let me be
I've tried to find a pure love so dearly
Death came by, his vengeance was deadly

For it killed all the love that lived within me
Forcing me to pretend with forceful decree
To love whom ever came to give love to me
So, death would not cometh, for now I am free

Jaime A Gonzalez
6-14-00

Emotional Collage

My heart resembles an emotional collage

Held together by the women in my life

The pieces are remnants of their love

Although fragmented my heart is whole

Liberally I gave my heart to each of them

But in going away small pieces were taken

Leaving me with a wounded, fractured heart

Needing mending, new loves would start

To heal that broken piece which was removed

Never been fully recovered it remained fragile

Mutilated and scarred and delicately afflicted

And like an emotional collage it has existed

Jaime A Gonzalez

11-13-01

Joaquin

It seems that just only yesterday

I felt you inside your mother's womb

I closed my eyes, and there you were

Heading off to school

So, I hugged you for a brief second

With a fatherly embrace

And in a single moment of time

You were off to school again

And so, I paused for just a moment

Wondering where all the years had gone

And discovered that my little boy

Had suddenly become a man

Jaime A. Gonzalez

4-5-05

A Brief Moment in Time

The calm sea appeared to be merging with the universe

In the immensity of the far and distant horizon

The tranquil waves caressing the white sands in perpetual motion

As I felt the refreshing breeze rushing through my cheeks

My thoughts return to you, to the day I first laid eyes on you

When the universe remained still for just an instant

When nothing else existed, only you

When your image became seared into my mind

For the rest of eternity

And it all occurred in a brief moment in the history of time

Jaime A Gonzalez

9-17-06

The Corner

It's almost nine forty-five and Blanco is getting ready for work
His shift begins at ten, he doesn't have to travel far
Several hundred feet or so, just outside the corner bar

He lived there all his life, on the concrete jungle in a corner road house
From his kitchen window, he saw how the world just moved about
Some cars would stop and someone would get out

A slight shake of hands, that no one cared about
The deal was made, the drugs he got for the money he gave
Back in the car he went, and with a sneaky smile he waved

Morning and night twenty-four hours a day
No matter the heat, no matter the rain
Someone was always there to supply the crave

Blanco got there on time every day
But this morning was different
Blanco by his mom was delayed

A slow car was moving, by the corner he dealt
Machine gun fire, was all that was heard
Bodies were running and bodies that fell

Blanco that morning was lucky as hell
It was his mother that stopped him
As he had survived with a story to tell

Don't hang on the corner, listen to me well
Bullets are flying and people are dying
Mothers are crying on the corner of hell

Jaime A. González
12-29-10

Traces of You

Don't think just because you're gone
I've forgotten about you
There are still traces of you in my bedroom
Traces of lipstick on my pillow case
And the aroma of your perfume lingers on

Did you not scream my name in ecstasy?
The night we made love 'till the sunrise
You were loving me like crazy
So why then do you say goodbye
I don't understand the reason why

There are traces of you in the house
There are traces of you on my sheets
There are traces of you in my heart
There are traces of you on my lips

Maybe you were playing with my heart
Perhaps you were messing with my mind
Maybe you are afraid to be loved
By someone who is tender
By someone who is kind

Yes, I was hurt by your leaving
My heart broke as you close the door
The tears ran as you drove away
Yet somehow I felt sorry for you
For my love was honest, my love was pure

There are traces of you in the house
There are traces of you on my sheets
There are traces of you in my heart
There are traces of you on my lips

So, if you find yourself wanting
In those cold and lonely nights
For someone to love and to hold you
Don't you dare call my number
Cause darling you've lost that right

I'd rather live with the memories
Of the good times, I share with you
The tender moments and those warm kisses
That still lingers on my lips
There are traces in my heart, traces of you

There are traces of you in the house
There are traces of you on my sheets
There are traces of you in my heart
There are traces of you on my lips

Jaime A. Gonzalez
12-26-10

The Fight

The vigorous and vernal lad took care of physical body
He ran, exercised and maintained a healthy living
Believing that his body was some kind of temple
He sculptured and chiseled it in the form of bodybuilding

His herculean physique was the envy of many men
The years of discipline training had surely come to light
Spending so much time in the arena of his own making
He never expected to be challenge to such a grueling fight

His opponent was cunning, ruthless and intimidating
Not many had dare to look at him straight in his eyes
Even though he had been defeated several times before
Many of the strong men tremble at the presence of his size

No one desired to challenge him for he did the challenging
He sets the times, he picks the place, and he picks his opponents
So today his eyes were fixed on young atlas as his contender
The young man doesn't have a clue for his challenger's resentments

The fight was scheduled downtown in the great metropolitan area
The challenger and his opponent were ready to make their statements
The first round was very intense and both fighters were weakened
By the cleverly defensive tactics of the two courageous contestants

Round one came to a close and while they waited for the second
It seemed like an eternity, for both of them gave it their all
The bell sounded and the two fighters came out swinging
Neither one wanted to back down, as each strike took its toll

The second round was becoming more vicious than the first
For the experience fighter seemed more resilient and unwavering
But the younger man had the strength and an indestructible will
Going toe to toe trading blow by blow waiting for the bell to ring

Each fighter was totally exhausted waiting in opposite's corners
Staring at each other dreading the moment round three would begin
Back in the center of the square round three was on its way
No one is backing down but to give up at this moment would be a sin

The athletic young man is finding himself in the fight of his life
And his challenger knows it, with every counter hit he eerily grins
For the young atlas is staggering and seems to be slowing down
He tries with one last effort but he fails and falls, cancer wins

Jaime A Gonzalez
7-3-10

The Fifth of November

Remember, remember of course I remember that fifth of November
When half past the hour of noon, this world you'd reached
For I was young as a father but younger was she
The young girl who bore you and who rocked you to sleep

So, gentle and fragile in our arms you would be
For we were young as your parents, young ones indeed
So, we learned how to hold and to bathe you we did
You were my first born; God knows how much I love thee

Every fifth of November, through the years I remember
That child that was born and made a father of me
And the time that was passing, there was no news of this
And how often I wonder, how your face it would be

One day on '94 at mothers, a postcard I'd received
Searching you were, for a person who would have been
Living in Riverside, California where you were conceived
With the card in my hand, I quietly began to weep

The years that had passed were many you see
Our encounter that evening was not a success
I failed to take advantage of our meeting you know
And for that I was guilty and I surely confess

And just like the wind you suddenly vanished
For I heard you were very disappointed in me
So, with the years once again, I got punished
Then I got the courage, and contact you, I did

This time our meeting was a good one indeed
I'd move heaven and earth to see you again
You are my daughter; we are the same you see
You carry my blood and you are my seed

So, did I remember that fifth of November?
You can rest assure that I certainly did
For every day that had passed, I surely agree
Yosha, you should know, that I've always love thee.

Jaime A Gonzalez
11-5-10

A Solitary Candle Sat

Through the frigid, iced frosted window
Glimmering upon a lonely table top
A solitary candle burning sat, flickering
Upon the boards of an old country shack.

As the wind swept through the naked trees,
An eerie sound engulfed the desolate plain.
The howling wolves send chills into my inner soul
And a sense of desolation tried to drive me insane.

While my gazed fell upon your sleeping body
Illuminated only by the dancing flame
My thoughts betrayed you with another lover
Whose passionate kisses I could hardly tame.

I will end this struggle at dawn's first light
Must say good bye to those satin lips
That stole my soul and held me captive
When pressed against mines, my life they grip

My farewell was weak, but very stern
My spoken words you did not believe
Your teary blue eyes tore my heart
Because my leaving, you could not conceive.

While I was home I joined the guards
To fight a war, I did not understand
Neither you nor my wife was aware of this
I was forgotten in time in a desolate wasteland.

Many years had passed; I became fragile and grey
Never again seeing those eyes of blue and hair of gold
Till one day from a transit bus, I saw you pass
I tried to reach out to you, but my heart became cold.

Jaime A Gonzalez
12-3-11

Mary Merlene

Your name was change after you were born
The name was already picked is what I mean
Someone went against your mother's wishes
For your name was supposed to be Mei Lynn

I was also not supposed to date your mother
For it was against some rule I was told
But also, because dating a pregnant girl
It just didn't seem right, it didn't fit the mold

You became my little girl from the very beginning
I was not your biological father as I was often told
But that didn't stop me from loving you like I do
For there's a chamber within my heart that you hold

I can still see that little girl playing with her blue doll house
Running on her tippy toes across that wooden floor
Reaching for the things you weren't supposed to grab
But I'll always treasure those memories for evermore

Jaime A Gonzalez
12-8-13

Second Guessing Life

The cool water of the Atlantic is gently rinsing my feet
As I sit on a green canvas folding chair at the water line
I am focus at a distance where the sea meets the sky
I watch in a total trance as my mind travels back in time

As I replay different scenes from my past life
Stopping at different intervals for mere seconds
Evaluating certain faults and mistakes I've made
Condemning myself for decisions I had beckoned

Wondering if I could relive my whole life once again
Would I dare to change the road I had traveled on?
But if I did then so many lives would not exist
What would happen to my daughters and my sons?

One thing is clear I can try to change or control my fate
Then I know the outcome could very well be different
So, whatever new road I may choose to travel upon
No matter the decision my destiny will remain permanent

Then I hear the sounds of children playing at the shore
Suddenly my wondering mind returns and I am back to reality
I then see a little boy and a little girl so cheerfully playing
Immediately I think of my children whom I love so greatly

It is then I realize that fate and destiny they don't really matter
That what is important is where in life I find myself today
To treasure where time has brought me thus far
And not worry about past things and the acts of yesterday

Jaime A Gonzalez
6-11-14

Twenty-Six Letters

Twenty-six letters, characters which by themselves have no meaning
Harmonized into an infantile song taught to children for learning
Letters that when arrange into proper sequence can communicate
Beautiful sounding words which can melt the heart of any young woman
And can also destroy that heart, to the point that it would never recover

Vocalizing these letters, we can elevate our words up to the highest heaven
And we can also arrange them to curse someone to the very pits of hell
We can build or we can destroy the inner most emotions of the human soul
The tongue sets these words into motion, so let us use these twenty-six letters
To heal broken hearts, comfort the downtrodden and give hope to the depressed
Let us use these twenty-six letters to build not to destroy to love not to hate
To bless not to curse to create friendships not enemies.
Twenty-six letters the foundation of our English vocabulary
Let us use these letters very carefully and very wise.

Jaime A Gonzalez

12-25-16

Unfinished Waltz

So why haven't we danced yet?
"Because you haven't asked me, was the reply
So, we danced and we danced that night
Until your loving heart became mines

Your gorgeous smile captured my love
And the sound of your laughter revived my soul
You stole my heart and merged it with yours
And the two hearts became one as a whole

You completed my soul when we were together
For every breath you took, I breathed twice
Because you were giving me part of yourself
Unselfishly every single day of your precious life

A short time has passed since you've been gone
In the eyes of family and friends it's been a long time
But for me it happens again every single morning
As I wake up and the nightmare begins with me crying

The grief I feel is greater today than on April sixteen
You were my joy, my lover, my wife and my friend
Twenty-four years of marriage and your smile still melted my heart
How can I live without you my love, I guess I'll just have to pretend

This sorrow has been taking over most of my daily life
I see your image every evening when I lay down
And I see it again each morning when I arise
For I feel your presence and it's all around

My love I miss you so much that it hurts me to breath
My heart aches so bad, so I'll have to tell you now
About the wasted seconds and minutes that I let passed by
So now you're gone, living without you I just don't know how

So, another tomorrow comes, I see no end to my sorrow
It's a reoccurring nightmare that never seem to end
It replays that day over and over in an endless loop
Dear Lord heal my heart, heal my sorrow help me mend

I know that many people mean well by their encouragement
And it makes me feel good for just a small period of time
But after all is calm and everyone has gone
I am left with this emptiness in my solitude at bedtime

What I wouldn't give now, to hear you laugh once again
What I wouldn't give, to hold you in my arms just once
What I wouldn't give, to kiss your sweet lips once again
What I wouldn't give, to have one last dance

Jaime A Gonzalez
4-16-14

Lost Love

I've talk with you before about many things
We joked and played games together
You made fun of my long hippy hair
But we laughed and it all seemed better

Till one day from the beach barefooted you came
Wet cutoff jeans and plaited shirt tie at the waist
At first it was nothing but then a second glanced
I saw you for the first time and my heart just raced

How nervous I became every time you got close
Being afraid to talk with you, I did not understand
I was just eighteen and you were young
What was that feeling, was I in a dreamland

Some time passed so I asked for your hand
Engaged we became and made wedding plans
Then the note you gave me sent me away
I became nauseous with heart aches and pain

Two days a week to your house I would go
While I patiently waited to see you walk by
You would pass and would not uttered a word
My eyes were relieved but my heart secretly cried

How much I loved you as it hurt not to say so
But I was glad to see your image once more
It was like seen a goddess in pure motion
So, I came to treasure those moments evermore

So, this scene continues for over a year or so
I come to gaze upon you but we did not speak
Seeing you would keep my love alive
Knowing you were there was all I could seek

I cannot remember how we came together again
But it must have been the persistence in me
When I held you in my arms my eyes became a fountain
As my heart melted with love from deep within me

As I left to serve and defend my country
How sad and lonely we both became
But I was weak and fell in the arms of another
As I betrayed the love I fought so hard gain

The hurt I caused you was unforgivable
As I fell prey to the same kind of pain
Can I dare and try to win you back?
Could I be that crazy or just insane?

So, I fought for your heart and won you again
A new engagement and new ring I gave to you
Making plans for a wedding the both of us were
When news I got that broke my heart in two

For the girl, I betrayed you with was now with child
I went desperately crazy not knowing what to do
How could I tell you and destroy you once again?
The fear of tearing your heart by confessing it to you

So, I sought council on the way it should be handle
Weighing in the possibility and holding on to you
So, I found the nerves and told you the whole truth
I could have never imagined what it did to you

I can still see your face whenever I relive this event
As it still hunt's me the pain that I caused you again
Seeing you crying loudly and laughing at the same time
It was laughter of unbelievable sadness and pain

Whenever I speak about that dreadful evening
Remembering that day, it can hardly be contained
As my voice cracks up and I become very emotional
While a disgusting feeling comes, and fills me with disdain

You were wise beyond your years on what you said
Forget about our love for you must be a father first
Leave and take care of that child and hold no regrets
For our true love was doomed and forever cursed

I tried to live up, to your expectations of me
Married the girl, and a beautiful daughter came
Happiness did not live there and like you I was betrayed
I lived your laughter of unbelievable sadness and pain

Returned home to find you had been married
Like me happiness did not exist in your home neither
Seeing you from a distant was repeated once again
But after four years my love for you was not alter

It was physically impossible not to run into you
As my brother was married to your sister and all
The pain of being so close to the ones we loved
As I held you with my eyes and kissed you with my soul

This time for fear your husband took you away
Not letting me at least look upon you once again
As we looked into each other's eyes without saying a word
In silence, Good bye my love, good bye 'till I see you again

Many years past just hearing about you from time to time
Seventeen years had passed without a glimpse of you
'Till one day at my brother's house I got a surprise
There was a young lady there who was a split image of you

I became frozen in time, as it was the image I had of you
Dropping the coffee cup from my hands as it broke in two
Exclaiming out at loud, how is it possible, oh my God
As your daughter at seventeen looked exactly as you

Walking towards me she came smiling just like you
As she rushed to put her arms around me and said
You must be the man that would have been my father
I could not contain my tears as my heart slowly bled

Although many years have passed one thing remains
A soul mate's love will never die or be put to rest
We were physically together for only two years
But emotionally we are bound for eternity's test

Even though we never got married or lived together
There is a love that still lives deep inside my soul
That no one or anything has been able to claim
Twas born for one purpose, and it was yours to hold

So, I've lived my life with the memory of our love
Perhaps you've lived your life with the same downfall
Treasuring the lost love that could have been
Having you in my memory, is better than not having you at all

Jaime A Gonzalez
3-22-14

A Gleaming Star in the Fog

You were that radiant star who illuminated the way
That guided the steps that led me into your heart
You were the one who'd awaken the passion
That felled dormant during a cruel and tragic past

You were that great compassion who relieved the pain
That was slowly consuming my inner being
You were the spark who ignited my dying love
That lit the flame which began to warm my soul

You were the robe that covered my frigid body
That melted the glacier which surrounded my heart
You were the essence who gave life to a forgotten being
That had been discarded and found salvation in your arms

You were the oasis where I drank the fresh water
That alleviated the thirst that existed in my soul
You were the owner of those sweet and tender lips
That moisturized my own with a soft and velvet kiss

You were the refuge where I found the repose
That my exhausted body searched and longed for
You were that lovely woman who shared her soul
That her most wanting desire was only to be loved

You began to uncovered your voluptuous body
That instantly set my cold frigid heart on fire
You were converted into a carnal masterpiece
That was being exhibited on a satin canvas

We made lustful love like savage cats in the wild
That were scratching and moaning in sweet ecstasy
We became a pair of two sensuous and crazed lovers
That excitedly reached the passion in explosive climax

We lived a wondrous love story that so sadly culminated
That it may have been compared to an ancient fairy tale
We had a marvelous relationship with an impossible love
Our love truly existed in this vast and grandiose universe

Jaime A Gonzalez
3-10-14

And the Enemy Moves In

Stealth-fully and viciously he silently moved in
In a pleasurable atmosphere, he settles deep within
Like a thief in the night he lays there in wait
Unhurried and unworried planning to migrate

He lays there in silence unnoticeable to many
For an alien visitor, his tenacity is very eerie
The effects of his actions flow up to the surface
But by this time the defenses are mostly useless

Introducing a more docile enemy to take a stand
Enemy of my enemy we'll use an illegal contraband
In comes cannabis sativa to take control of the torment
Opening flood gates of chemicals without consequent

While getting addicted to marijuana, pain pills and all
The pain being inflicted send love ones towards a pitfall
Pointing fingers and accusations in a continues brawl
Forgetting we are defenseless on another's persons fall

We see our love ones wasting away before our very eyes
Punishing ourselves, while being emotionally crucified
Even with the choices they made, we still carry their pain inside
Unable to help them break the addiction we often ask God, Why?

Why is this happening to our dearest and loving child
With this crazed obsession while the body is being defiled
We would gladly exchange places and it would be worthwhile
Carrying this enemy to the portals of hell and be forever exiled

Jaime A Gonzalez
4-25-17

Life O' Life

Life o' life how many blows have thou launched on my life's journey
   I don't remember asking to be here, never the less here I am
   But early in mine own infancy you did mentally scarred me
  Should I have censure you for branding me into this sociogram?

Painful memories helped to create the strength that is within me today
If it had not been so, I do believe I would have perished in solitude
I've learned to turn tragedy into a more enduring desire to survive
And above all things considered, I've endured this emotional prelude

Yet fate has always found a way to come at me from different angles
Many times, invisibly cloaked, other times directly straight to my eyes
Mocking me, challenging my resolve, attempting to destroy my spirit
Life o' life when will you learn, by your actions my essence is magnified

For thou did send that grim reaper to take away my teenaged son
It wasn't enough for you to have extinguished the loves I've had
Creating and destroying seems like a cruel way for your time to pass
So now hovering over my daughter, is that specter in a rebellious dyad

Life o' life how many more darts in my direction would thou willfully cast
Being emotionally and spiritually scarred my faith I've always kept
You've tried your best to destroy that spark which in my soul does rests
  Although I've concealed that pain I confess, I have also secretly wept

                Jaime A Gonzalez
                     5-3-17

A Matter of Fate

Returning to my past through photographs, scrapbooks and journals
I glanced upon the face and the beauty that enslave my soul
With a luscious tender smile mingled with the gleam of her eyes
My life became hers, for her youthful spirit made me whole

Refreshing it was to see the face which gained the love I gave to her
That alluring smile captured on that faded photograph of yesterday
So many memories were ignited and rushing forth they came
Reviving those forgotten emotions which I carefully had put away

With tear filled eyes remembering the times we lived for each other
Planning our future for a lifetime of happiness yet to unfold
The kind of car, the type of house, the number of children to be born
Plans that were easy to make for the love we had was so bold

So now the years have passed and that love we had, has faded away
Yet it's still living as a silent relic deep in our heart's reserved
For we now live our separate lives, with partners we call our own
For fate didn't grant us what we wanted, it only gave us what we deserved

Jaime A Gonzalez
9-17-17

This Old Soul

I feel I possess a very old soul inside this physical body
That's constantly looking for a love which has been lost
Trying to replicate those latent emotions for years past
I ask myself how many incarnations this soul has crossed

Looking for a loved soul which was lost centuries ago
Hoping to find that one love in a new incarnated being
So, I try again and again but it just isn't so
These relationships only exist to give me temporary feeling

In how many lifetimes have I attempted this unending quest
For I have glimpses of Victorian era of northern Spain
To the highlands of western Europe and the deserts of USA
How far has this soul traveled searching for that love to reclaim

Through space and time did my old soul hath traveled
Attempting to correct the wrongs of possible mistakes
Only to lose that love every time it was undertaken
Where will my next incarnation be when my soul reawakes

Jaime A Gonzalez
12-26-17

Thank You for Leaving Me

I remember how much I suffered when you left me

I felt like the weight of the world was falling upon me

As if the gravity of the planet had suddenly doubled

The pain and pressure I felt in my heart had me troubled

I desperately looked for ways to control my sanity

The loneliness and despair were causing me atrophy

I tried to maintain a new attitude, positive and pure

It forced me to face my hidden demons in search of a cure

I relived those bitter moments that on your soul I had planted

The humiliation, pain that I've caused you wasn't warranted

I traveled to dark, unknown places of spiritual damnation

It was there that I discovered my strength and my salvation

Realizing that it was that specific time, where I needed to be

You saved my life, and I wanted to thank you, for leaving me

Jaime A Gonzalez

12-16-18

My Christmas Shirt

The other day while trying to make room in the closet
I came across an old shirt, I thought I had thrown away
A red plaited long sleeve flannel shirt with dark lines
Suddenly memories rushed forth to some happy times

Remembering the person who once gave that shirt to me
Many years ago, as I recalled, on a snowy winter's night
A perfect gift that made me smile and filled my heart with bliss
As I looked deep into your eyes and thanked you with a kiss

To my utter surprise, it was what I found in the pocket within
T'was a black and white photograph from a photo booth machine
Of you making these weird faces which made me laugh again
Sending my thoughts to the past, as I was instantly entertained

So easy our minds break the laws of physics to travel back in time
Standing in the closet, my mind is in another state, another time
Then returning to the present my thoughts become more alert
Realizing my life has been good, I smile as I hug my Christmas shirt.

Jaime A Gonzalez
12-22-18

Going Off The Furrow

Eat drink and be merry, let us celebrate for the night is still young
How many of us have uttered those same words one time or another?
Eventually removing the word eat, now we are only merely drinking
Waiting for Friday's work day to end, cause that's all we've been thinking

Trying to get home, giving the wife a quick kiss on the way to the kitchen
Open the fridge and there she is eagerly waiting for you to consume her
She has become the object of your secret desires, taking her to your lips
You completely drained the life out of her in several continuous sips

Now you have arrived, finding more pleasure in the mouth of a bottle
Than a soft kiss from your wife, oblivious of how far you have traveled
While everything around your home is rapidly falling to the ground
Arguments, fights and the teen age kids on the streets running around

Planning for a Saturday picnic, the inebriants are first to go in the cooler
For it has now become the most important commodity in your life
The outing is just a peace offering for the chaos created the previous night
Pretending that all is fine because you can't remember there was even a fight

Being morphed into this bibulous individual you never had imagined
Knowing that your job is the means to support the habit, you're faithful
Coming out of a stupor you realize you've lost everything in your life
There's silence, things look different, the kids are gone and so is the wife

You have tried rehabs several times, but they never seem to work
Perhaps you thought you would never lose the ones who cared
So, you figured, "I could consume as much liquor as I can afford"
With no one to interfere you have enough booze in places stored

Then one day in the morning hours the spiders begin to terrorize you
The whole room is infested with them, on the walls and on the bed
You screamed like a raving lunatic get them off me, someone please
Delusional parasitosis has now settled in, it's now become your disease

Running around sifting through empty bottles looking for liquid residue
Something to take the proverbial edge off and keep the insects at bay
Suddenly you find a half a bottle, making you the richest man on earth
It has come to this; five fingers of ethanol it's all that your life is worth

Jaime A Gonzalez

12-31-18

Jaime Gonzalez

Jaime Gonzalez was born in the highlands of the Isle of Puerto Rico, and at the age of twelve, he moved to mainland USA where he grew up in Philadelphia. After graduating from school, he joined the US Marine Corps and served at Twenty-nine Palms, California. It was there that Jaime fell in love with the Mojave Desert and its treeless mountains. After a few years living in California, Jaime returned to Philadelphia and decided to join the Philadelphia Police Department serving faithfully for thirty years. At the same time, he became a member of the PA Army National Guard reserve. After retiring from the police force, Jaime promised himself never to wear another uniform again. However, when Jaime moved to Daytona Beach, Florida, he accepted a position as a Campus Safety Officer with Embry-Riddle Aeronautical University where he still works after eleven years. Jaime enjoys interacting with the student community and serves as the Crime Prevention Coordinator. It appears that throughout his lifetime Jaime has chosen professions of service to humanity. It is what he calls having "a servant's heart."

www.ingramcontent.com/pod-product-compliance
Lightning Source LLC
Chambersburg PA
CBHW031653040426
42453CB00006B/296